THE
FARTHER
SHORE

THE
FARTHER
SHORE

Poems by

PAUL KANE

with a note by Richard Howard

GEORGE BRAZILLER

New York

Some of these poems have previously appeared in the following periodicals to whose editors grateful acknowledgment is made: *The Adelaide Review, The Age Monthly Review, The American Review, Antithesis, Central Park, Grand Street, Meanjin, The New Republic, Scripsi, The Sewanee Review, Shenandoah.*

Published in the United States in 1989 by George Braziller, Inc.

Copyright © 1989 Paul Kane
All rights reserved.

For information address the publisher:
George Braziller, Inc.
60 Madison Avenue
New York, NY 10010

Library of Congress Cataloging-in-Publication Data

Kane, Paul, 1950–
The farther shore.
I. Title.
PS3561.A4715F37 1989   811'.54   88-7550
ISBN 0-8076-1216-2
ISBN 0-8076-1211-1 cl.

Printed in the United States of America
First Printing

LIBRARY
The University of Texas
at San Antonio

In Memoriam:

I. K. and W. A. N.

Ripae ulterioris amore

—Virgil

CONTENTS

III

A NOTE ON PAUL KANE

. . . little boulevards
of phrases become the avenues of approach

When a new poet beguiles us so readily, *without apparent effort,* by the charm of his diction, by the aspiring rise and the dying fall, by what Hopkins would call the *carol* of his voice moving back and forth between gentle margins, we suspect—as I began to suspect when I noticed Mr. Kane's poems some years ago, in the easy evanescence of a university milieu, then of magazine verse—that we are being deceived, toyed with, charmed in the sinister sense of the operation, as a bird is charmed by a serpent. Nothing this deliberately amiable can be so amiable as all that: such seductions must be paid for, accredited by what this poet cunningly identifies as "significant pain."

It would seem at first that we are being invited to enjoy "a season of no regret, an/afternoon beyond compulsion." So formidable are the accomplishments of this latest student of all the nostalgias that for once we appear to be in the presence—and ever so happy to be there, revelling even, if that is not too vehement a word for our satisfactions—of an art without the usual exactions, without that clutch upon our efforts of attention which is the regnant character of *the modern* in its dread avatar among us. As if the poet were merely casting into the cool inscriptions which are his gift and his gaud (his *guile,* I have called it) our intransitive contemplation, producing from a collection of accidents, cryptically presented, a design of reverential rhetoric which but stands, stock still, a monument. But once we have read through his collection, his series, his *structure,* we learn more, we think better of ourselves for discerning that these poems of "older travels, other travails," of "a pastoral world [that] is forever past," are not mere blandishments, adorable winding sheets around our reassurance. Rather, it seems to me, they are, ultimately, quite insistent presentments of that mortal energy of alternation which for Paul Kane constitutes what it is to be "human: the flood/and withdrawal of the tide." Repeatedly the figure occurs:

> And no misgivings could mar this moment—
>   the very waves, beating the shore, withdraw
> in foaming undertow and carry with the tide:
>   exhausted, redeemed; exhausted, redeemed.
> It is the fever of our lives that we
>   compel the sudden changes and all the while
> ache with an alien solitude, knowing what
>   changes us flows from a sea beyond change.

And again, in the title poem where Kane declares we have not fallen, we are falling still, sliding down the waves forever, he offers that program of systole and diastole which is our anatomy, our fate:

> The far shore cries out with the voices of leaves
> whirled in the wind: "farther, farther," the sound
> in the rustle lifts, dies down and lifts again.

We are taken back to Shakespeare's *ebbed man,* and to the sense that the self is never immune to a sort of vegetable repetition-compulsion,

> this common body,
> like to a vagabond flag upon the stream,
> goes to and back, lackeying the varying tide,
> to rot itself with motion.

But attend how lovingly this anything-but-innocent voyager offers us the booty of his helplessness ("The Whores of Algeciras," "Canada," even his pretended, his projected, his *dramatized* helplessness in "Mr. Emerson Assisted on His Walk"); not that he is a Tiresias-figure—far from it! He has not yet eroded his illusions, his sexuality (are they the same?), but he has premonitions, he has doubts: "the past has yet to happen—these are figments of presence."

And if it seems to me that on one occasion certainly Kane goes past premonitions into the region of prophecy (in the alarming poem "Stellar Junk," where he declares in a panic beyond the personal "We hope it will end there. We are looking/forward to uncreation, to beyond our own time"), the point to loiter upon, as if it were no more than a palm extended, is the vivid ease of these semblances: "we live in the mirror world of our waking, the crystal/refractions, the prison of our prism." This poetry makes itself "easy" on us so that we will the more efficiently understand what is arduous, what is intolerable; so that we will turn the poet's own words back upon him, declaring:

> We search the sound of what you say,
> We wish to come close to what you see . . .

—RICHARD HOWARD

I

THE FARTHER SHORE

In the beginning all the World was America.
—JOHN LOCKE

On the emigrant wharf, milling like birds
flocking in the shallows, the people wait.
But the sea is wider than a dream of the sea,
and freedom a coin on the tongue of the living.
The far shore cries out with the voices of leaves
whirled in the wind: "farther, farther," the sound
in the rustle lifts, dies down and lifts again.

We have not fallen, it seems, we are falling still,
sliding down the waves forever breaking forward
in time, our time. Blessèd be the "Arbella."
What craft is this, that we accommodate such
motions, such destinies? The gods keep covenants
men break in half; demi-gods rule their children.
"Farther, farther," beckons the city on the hill.

At the branching of the waters, we ask what heresy
are we moved by, that the current should run so strong?
The light, composite, becomes darkness; the sun
on the waves is blindingly white to our eyes.
As the world comes closer, the shores of America
recede—farther, farther. Across the removing sea,
we are only the vessels of ourselves, our world.

CANADA

When Jacques Cartier passed with his three small ships
And his fifty men through the Strait of Belle Isle,
And the smiling whales were spouting and rolling
In the broad salt-bay, and the sun was hot,

For it was the tenth of August, a martyr's day,
Did he turn then and think of Saint Lawrence who made sport
Of his pain, grilled on that slow fire of death?
And later, when the water flowed fresher

Near the mouth of the Saguenay and the singing whales
Receded, did Cartier in the morning haze
Look at the steep shores and the crowds of gannets,
And, in the deep mingle of sound and river-smell,

Look again, and see his life as something obdurate?
The white bears that swam, the scattered puffins at dusk,
The herons that glide so slowly, might all have seemed
Beautiful to the Breton pilot, but closer

To his reckoning were the red cliffs, the sharp
Rocks, the waterfalls that burst to the shore
And fed the sea. He was careful to have prayers
In the morning and again in the evening, for

The murmurous passages of the sea give rise
To an echo of redemption—human: the flood
And withdrawal of the tide and her winds.
Yes, there was much that could touch his French purposes:

The banks of cod, the tall straight spruce, and of course
The Indians, those Hurons of Donnacoma
With their wild ingratiating stories of gold,
And the furs off their backs, the corn, the hot bread,

The sick and the old coming to be healed,
And the young women rubbing their arms and running
Into the woods. These were of his order.
And of the luminous nights, and the range

Upon range of mountains—the immensity
Really—there was nothing Cartier could do but see it
As something savage, something that reduced himself
And enlarged the stars and the portion of him

That beating suddenly with life, recognized his existing
As far away from his knowing, as foreign
As the vast village he called Canada is
To the constellations that guided him there.

ROCK CREEK CEMETERY:
WASHINGTON D.C.

*He supposed its meaning to be the one
commonplace about it—*
—HENRY ADAMS on *Grief,* the memorial
to his wife, by Saint-Gaudens

It is not in Lafayette Park, nor near
the Mall, where the Monument—kneeling down—
is blackened with names, half-buried in earth.

The plot-site, ringed with a crown of holly,
grows in upon itself, like obsession.
Here, you are the third person, singular.

The Virgin, the Dynamo come to Grief:
she sits in a posture impossible
to hold too long. Hooded bronze, shrouded eyes.

We must seek to live two separate lives,
he said, and watched his neighbors purchase pain.
Grief, removed to Lafayette Park, looks on.

MR. EMERSON ASSISTED ON
HIS WALK

Bush
Concord, 1872

In a way, William, I had hoped you wouldn't come:
    An old man fears most his best friends.
Here, turn here, help me along down to the pear trees.
    We outlive ourselves. The commonest
Object, the most familiar face, all suddenly
    Stand before us as if it were
The first day in Paradise: nameless and foreign.
    This grammar comes unglued, in time—

Nothing sticks together, especially our speech.
    We sit serenely dumb. Oh, the mind
Is quick, but the words are slow to form, no longer
    Willing to dance upon the tongue.
So you see, I would rather be quiescent
    And forgo the solicitude
Of society, than endure those eager
    Countenances of friends who hang

Precipitously at the edge of my teetering
    Sentences, while I abruptly
Am visited by the two facts of existence:
    I and the Abyss! It is that
Which drives me to an husbandman—at least my pears
    Will flourish without a flourish,
And give a poor man some taste of simplicity,
    Something that grows from the roots up.

But why should that, just now, stir this vague rumor of
    A memory? Have I forgotten
Some resolution, some important matter?
    I cannot, will not remember!
Just so, my friend, it's like losing your place in a book,
    Or neglecting to turn the page.
But look, see how the sun glimmers on the Bartletts,
    On the Napoleons, golden,

Yes? Napoleons . . . There's that itch again. Ah, yes.
    Carlyle has sent a letter. There now,
We can pass it by. Oh, but not these Flemish Beauties!
    Do I rave? I suppose one pays
For a hobby by becoming a bore—and there's
    No assurance one won't simply
Stumble against some opening in the Void, like
    The oblivious chemist who

Annihilates himself and hardly knows the difference.
    We take these days as they come,
And what we bear is often all we can bear, for now:
    Life never lessens, it's a
Daily defeat, William, a triumph of circumstance
    Over conscience . . . but not for
Nothing—we drink from an endless
    Well of anguish, and are refreshed.

Wait a moment here, I think we are going wrong:
    The house is in that direction.
No? Well, I'm certain I know my own grounds, and we
    Most likely will miss our supper.
But if you insist . . . There was a time, before "Bush"
    Burned last July, when a cow-bell
Would announce the occasion. It's no longer
    Felicitous—we have other ways now.

And with what huge fervor that fire burned! It was
   The arson of Nature, meant to
Drive me off her threshold. I don't know what was more
   Glorious that morning, the sun
Coming up blazing yellow, or the house going
   Down all red-hot timbers and great
Leaps of flame—I felt like the orphan of Spirit
   Suspended between two burning worlds.

And standing there with a strange disinterest, some voice
   Of the wind whispered to my ear,
"Fire makes and unmakes, fire sustains." And since then,
   I walk from room to room with constant
Curiosity, as would some diligent
   Stranger to a foreign palace.
But, I say, we're going towards the barn, not the house.
   Perhaps. Certainty shuns me these days.

And yet, we would forget night and day, sky and stars,
   If we could ransom our knowledge
For a vision, to shed this stubborn sleep of flesh.
   This, this nature is a jealous god—
She does not give over her bonds of affection
   Easily: we pay with our life.
Still . . . My heavens! There's the house, there's "Bush" itself!
   Ah, splendid. The situation

Was most urgent and required a miracle:
   The house has simply pirouetted
And settled on the other side of the garden!
   Come then, remind me to show you
That letter Carlyle sent, poor man: this whole world
   Of nonsense torments him to despair.
But you shall read it by the fire. Ellen, I think,
   Has cooked some pears for our pleasure.

A PAINTING, PERHAPS

Lithe, long, her white dress clings
as she leans on the gateway post,
hat in hand, the red band trailing,
the sunlight a matter of shadow.

She is about to speak. The man
sits in a wicker chair, watching.
He listens with foreknowledge of
what she will say. So little to tell.

It is a garden beside a house,
nasturtiums entangle one another.
It is a season of no regret, an
afternoon beyond compulsion.

The eye is led down the lane
to a scene the body desires:
the discrete moment of still-life
in a cinematic whirr of frames.

So little to go on. What color means,
color means that. The old story.
A woman by a gate, a man who
listens. We know how it ends.

LADY WITH A FALCON:
A TAPESTRY

She is a woman given to symbols: the falcon
on her left hand, a private sorrow, weathering;
the small rabbits that "populate the oak bushes"
fleet, diligent, in the service of propensity:
signs of a red rejection, in passionless blue.
It is a gesture of renown to look so struck,
the head bent so with a crown of grief,
what eminence fills her empty hand? And the men,
in Arras, who wove her at the high-warp loom,
what could they feel for the finery, for the silk,
the wool, and tragic face? This was the dream that
troubled them, after so many copies of the "noble couple,"
this fourth Fate, this image Penelope left in air,
unravelling into hopelessness the high-bred
solitude of a life shaken by knowledge of others,
by noble couples stirring the waters with a stick.
This was the dream that troubled them, and some
stone cloister or gallery of fine things
stands accused—high corridors sound
the scraping and shuffling of small bones,
the hawk and falcon learn of the bat,
and many people, uncertain people, pass
the dolorous Lady with the jewelled head.
Now the weavers falter, weary of their tapestry,
caught in the shuttle of necessity, they
beat down the threads, but the image still
rises, troubled in the darkening grove—they feel
with sensitive hands textures of a dream
forsworn, how it hovers over the heavy head,
light, now dark, now winding up the woven stair,
high where the falcon rings, where fear

hangs, pity hangs—hangs, in reproach of time,
in the blue grid of the taut sky,
the warp, the weft of significant pain.

SEQUINS

And so to conclude, he says, and pauses.
Looking up, out the window, into distance,
the river, flat in the background, moves
forward, embellished, displaying a sequined hem.
The monotonous shadows around take edge,
the sun lights up a hydrant on the lawn,
sight alters within his eyes, focusing
the convergences of a thought: it's clear,
he is wrong, others right; for otherwise
locality fails—or rather, it succeeds
just where his own argument cannot.

Exactly then, in a city, uptown,
a woman in black, in a sequin dress, is
putting on her gloves—drinks before dinner,
another night out—when the lights below
flare up along the streets in late summer dusk
like shining thoughts, brilliant feelings.
It is a cool evening, autumnal,
the air as forgiving as tempered glass,
and her mirror smiles upon her smile
as something thrills along the edges of
her heart: she becomes her own desires.

At which moment, an old coin dealer, after
hours, pulls out an even older wooden tray
from an oak cabinet—his father's in fact—
removing two antique coins: the gold disks,
called zecchinos, or sequins, from the late
thirteenth century, Venetian, worth back then
about two dollars, are precious now—as
mementos—beyond the precisions of price.
Fingering the soft gold indentations

is like touching the hem of heaven. And
soon they will go to his daughter and son.

DEVICES

i

Take the stream as the emblem,
the one unvisited in the woods.
Notice the cascade of rocks—
they were always there, unseen,
until the stream uncovered them.

ii

Go to where the water rushes,
very steep. Do not look at the foam:
see the undisturbed current.
This may not merely figure.

iii

Or, if you wish, closely
watch the crash of water—
the single drops flung,
undifferentiated. When they enter
the stream again, exhale.

WINTER IS COMING

Pushing the prow, the waves wash by,
The tug-boat pulls the barge.
The air chills, and the sun is hot
On the face of the man piloting.
  Winter is coming, the dead leaves fall.

Shale and slate, the black mass riding,
Lies along the tow-line.
The islands pass, reds and browns,
And the fishermen hail the pilot:
  Winter is coming, the dead leaves fall.

Back at home, where the white crests
Do not foam, the wife sits weaving.
She is different, knows the small birds
And flowers of fall, dislikes the salt-sting.
  Winter is coming, the dead leaves fall.

The distance between is dying:
Seasons and sufferings,
By course, descend along the tow-lines
Of time, hover like terns, then sweep away.
  Winter is coming, the waves wash by.

NUOVA

Not that the wind was sad to see her go,
it just didn't want her to leave that way:
abrupt, hurried, without the prolonged good-bye.
But the mountain knew the weight of grief and held

the wind close to the contours of its wisdom
saying: let go, let her go where wind
never follows—where voices call
for the undeparted, words of the welcome

few—the home of human phrasing.
What the mountain understood the wind denied,
for it moved along the black roads gathering
sounds to search the hearts of people passing.

And despite the recognition that it found,
the resonance of pain, the resolute
self affirmed in the face of every loss,
she was gone to a place of departure.

DAY SAILOR

And when the wind failed he steadied
himself with sea-sounds: the jangle
of the rigging, the water slapping
the hull, the dull and languid murmur
of the waves—the sigh of his breath.

The little map gave ridiculous
directions—Dakar: 3,150 miles,
Cape Hope: 6,290 miles—while three
miles out, he criss-crossed the harbor,
thinking of shipwrecks off Nantucket.

He considered the victims, wished
himself to be thought a victim,
and admired the simplicity
of fate—or at least of fated lives,
the obvious ones—the way it

redefines the terms of life as pure
survival, how suddenly all is
altered by some freak concurrence.
And he knew he had the stuff of
failure, the capacity for "why?"

And he knew he should fail, and took
for a sign the coming wind curling
across the water: life would be short,
and when he died, his sigh would mix
with the wind, and circulate forever.

AN OLD POET IN HIS GARDEN

The midday heat advances, while morning lingers
in spruce shade, in an advocate breeze.
Languid as foxglove, he rests, makes an idyll
out of sunlight whitening like moonlight.
Birds keep their distance that once sang to him,
as he withdraws equally into equilibrium.
No fly disturbs the implacable countenance.

His books are a commonplace of the singular.
All his life he has wanted to silence time,
still the interminable tick of mortality,
stand for a solitary moment shining
with the glory of nihilation, the all of nothing.

Lately, he has taken up a tone, something
he heard in the garden: a melding of sounds,
with fragrances of the shade intermixing
sweet silences. Too elegiac in youth
to have much patience with age, he wonders
at the ease of his own timely translation.

He is not truly admired—his readers think only
of themselves. A secretary answers the mail,
has learnt his signature, as he has unlearnt
its character. To what end all this passion?
In the garden, an impasse passes, as he muses
on the day when the morning-glories opened.

THE GLASS FOREST

Hidden within the wet snow of the night,
An enchantment of ice glazes the near woods
To perfection of form. Now the hard light,
Refracted to a sky of jewels, floods

The sense and memory with reflections.
Skeletal trees clack in glassy bodies
Incarnating dreams of resurrections
In spring. But the ice, like minor melodies

Dissonant in the moment of crescendo,
Cracks, breaks, slides off into air—the free
Fall of unfrozen music. Incrusted snow
Shatters into shards the molt of the tree,

The bent boughs spring back, and their glittering
Vanishes. What is light, that trees should wish
To embrace it? And this cold splintering
Heart of desire, the second self of flesh?

In the glass forest, birds sing to themselves,
To the sun, which is the self of their song.
Shadowless, we enter the woods as ourselves
And fill with the radiance of one song.

II

EUROPE: FIVE POEMS

THE GARDEN WALL

Assolas House
County Cork

Here the stones, in accents of moss,
clung flowers and vines, speak of chance
in change—of falling down to build up—
of remains, removals, the residual seed:
the necessity of walls in a garden.
By the waterside rhododendrons grow.

Still, the stream seems not to move, and
the water is smooth as it washes the dam
and runs among the stones downstream.
In wind, blossoms, bits of grass float
backwards, against a deeper current,
as if in memory of a source.

The garden wall refuses memory, has no
knowledge of beginnings, knows only the
present hour—keeping in, keeping out—
in ruin, in completeness, while the stream
beside moves like time, unnoticed and
still, in reflecting surfaces of sky.

THE WHORES OF ALGECIRAS

Night, and the night sky clear, with so little moon
Gibraltar looms darker than the dark:
cavern-mouth, black tunnel the dreamer
descends finding the shape and image
of himself dreaming. Here no opening, here
the wide way barred, in protest, again.

Travelers of the road, we stop, digress,
and see a stranger approach. He will become
our story. Foreign, Spanish, he speaks,
accomplishes some English phrases, says,
Do you want some Coca, a glass of Coca?
Local color in the dark—we accept.

Keen, quick, he takes us winding ways
deep in the empty streets, past low-slung
habitations, slums of the one lamp.
A moment, and fear is the thirst for fear:
alleyway, door, the room, and the woman:
fat, old, marvellous, sits nodding. *Mama.*

Little table in little room, what do you offer,
something to drink? The girls come out.
In the streets of Europe, in Amsterdam, Paris, here,
stone pavings of hardened emotion lie as
a layer of life, sustaining, in body,
the people who live and walk the streets.

I, not of their city, decline: will choose to
wait outside for my friend, who chooses
the fat blonde, not the bony-haired
who sits by me, in nightgown, in perfume,

stroking my thigh, proficient in one phrase,
her one query, who is not beautiful,

who is not young, who is herself, who is
working tonight. The air grows heavy outside;
the gravelled street moans as I walk.
I would like a cigarette. Perhaps
the pimp—but his friend is not friendly,
smiles like a knife. Wants my money.

I give them pesetas. Pay for my life,
pay and withdraw, turn, and in the instant
of turning, hold my last breath, take my
last step, dissolve in configuration of
shadow and dust, thinking: *Here,*
they would pray to the Mother of God.

In the car, locked in attitudes of
remembrance, we hardly acknowledge each
other, as I drive to find a place to sleep,
somewhere near the border, something
close and not too dear. In Algeciras,
you pay the same for virtue as for vice.

SASSETTA ON ST. FRANCIS

Siena, 1451

How cold the bricks and dampened
  On the Porta Romana, and I lying there
As now I lie here, on my back.
  I die—stabbed through and through
By the sharp southwest wind—it is much
  The same to say "I live." Come, Lady Pain,
Wed me in the painless night. Can it be
  So quiet? I hear but sounds
Of my own making . . . not so before, times
  Antiphonal to a liturgy of voices—
Composing, drawing, painting all
  In response to feeling the voice
Sound in the heart. My mortgaged heart.
  And at Borgo San Sepolcro, there for
Bernardine, that life of St. Francis:
  Song of the painted trees, gold leaf
Of the morning light. Yet, no voice
  There, for that was I, Stephano Sassetta,
Transfixed, painting in oils, self-
  Anointed: it was my own life I saw,
My death I drew, and draw on now.
  Faith was the central panel—hope aside,
And beggars are never charitable, save him,
  Who felt discourteous in the presence
Of anyone poorer than himself. I made him mine.
  His ecstasy, his purity: my wretchedness,
My failing. How else? Draw no fine distinctions
  There, my lines are fate, my colors
Of the earth: the damned imagine bliss,
  The saints can image nothing. And do I

26

Worship the blank wall? To live
So far below the sky, with the weight
Of a ruined life, who will befriend you
But Brother Sun, Sister Moon? Who will redeem
But Lady Pain, mother of sweetness?

BY THE RUINS OF CARTHAGE
AT SUNSET

To Carthage I came, where there sang all around me in
my ears a cauldron of unholy loves.

— AUGUSTINE

The flat sky, cerise, moves west beyond the lighted sea:
splendid, magnanimous with its cavalcade of clouds,
indifferent to demise, untouched by all the importunities of
promise, it gathers winds to itself along the shore.

The shore no longer weeps on the margins, on the sand—
the sea's already taken what it wants, and returns
what it doesn't. No more of those ships, those departures—
no more a woman to make a history of good-bye.

All's leveled here—only the shadowed colosseum,
with its declivity of stairs, looks whole, though ruined.
The further down in you go, the more you find the lost
prospect, the faded carving, the mosses in the cracks.

The boy, our guide, is nervous, guarded. He does not like
our questions, he will not talk about himself, nor of
the men, the tall stones, who watch the people in the town.
It is dry: the sirocco blowing hot from the east.

Back in Rome, the wind will be more humid, unpleasant—
the people will say, it is the wind, the sirocco;
they will look out over the balustrade to the south
and feel again some turn of enmity in the blood.

In Tunis, in the old quarter, it is cool where the
market turns to an underground labyrinth of stalls, where

28

the dark men, in their frowns, will sell you everything they
do not value, for almost nothing at all. No one

expects a different chance, another fate. As at noon,
they pass the dish around, take what they need, and as it
only amounts to what it is, and no more, then no less:
there's no refrain from the burden of repetition.

It will be evening soon, dark. No one comes here at night.
There is really nothing much left to see, and the boy
is nervous, the ruin complete. Later, out at sea,
under red skies, someone watches a fire on the shore.

A LETTER FROM ERASMUS

My dear Hutten, is it not a measure
  Of worth that a man send some moiety
Of friendship in a spare hour of leisure—
  Say, but ten minutes of his society—

In the meager form of a letter?
  Are we to be met with a sullen silence—
For so I take it—who merely utter
  The truth without a mincing diffidence?

If I have offended in my remarks,
  It is a long begrudgement that you bear.
But perhaps I age like our patriarchs
  At Rome and grow ill-tempered from horsehair

Shirts festering with lice—for though I never
  Wear one, my own hair is thick enough, and
Wash in this foul water of Paris? Rather
  Bathe in a ditch or roll in some swampland!

I would welcome, indeed, the sulphur springs
  That flow so amply in *your* direction—
For, let me be frank, I itch from stockings
  On up, but most for some conversation.

So I ask you to forgive what possible
  Impetuosity as might proceed
From my pen—unchecked by my unstable
  Reason, so distraught from your own misdeed.

30

But let us turn to a matter more sweet,
   And leave off my peevish bickering,
For I hope, when I see you again, to greet
   Your hand with the splendid offering

Of a book, one I know you possess in part,
   But this is the whole of a wild wonder—
And, as you must have guessed, I will sport
   With you no more, for it is More's *amour*.

You have known it till now as *Nusquama*,
   But in Greek it shall be: *Utopia*.
I have often thought a panorama
   Of the distant blue of Britannia

(From a French boat) the most uplifting sight
   For a poor pummelled indigent scholar.
And as I speed in my travels at night,
   Trusting through the country the northern star,

Only stopping to taste the provisions
   Proffered, and not to dwell but where caution
And judgment and all the cold suspicions
   Of the road may be left without question

At the door—so is this book of Thomas More
   A haven for the bedraggled: bereaved,
As we are, by the ceaseless furor
   Of milking a he-goat into a sieve.

So highly do I recommend to you
   This Englishman, that nowhere will you find
A more perfected image of virtue,
   So sober and cheerful, severe and kind.

But allow me to come closer to my mark:
  You are acquainted with More, I know,
We are used to speak of him, and yet, apart
  From that happy genius of his, sorrow

Mounts upon his back and begins to bend
  His generosity to deep designs—
I sense a change, and my fears all tend
  In a downward direction, for what binds

My tongue from clucking of what it tastes
  In the wind is fear to cause his demise.
I see ahead. The real successor to Wolsey's place
  Will not be our Thomas More—the enterprise

Of that Henry is to wrap his regal
  Head in swaths of the cloth-of-gold of power,
And heads will bow or fall before that lethal
  Sweep. He will find less in his new Treasurer

Than he hopes or could find profit with.
  Never will a King command that conscience—
Royalty's pittance before the sovereign life
  Of a spirit charged with obedience.

There is a deep violence of purpose
  Which heaves and boils like swelling sulphurous
Mud in crater-holes of Vesuvius:
  I have seen how his hairshirt stains his dress.

Sir Thomas is all steadiness, but cold
  Fire runs in his blood—the King will warm it.
Ah, but now I touch the edge of his mold:
  It is sharp . . . he will not play the favorite,

He cannot be cast in anything less
　　Than the iron of a dungeon, or the gold
Of heaven—there is no mid-ground to rest
　　Upon, nor does he offer any foothold

To catch a view of that vertiginous
　　Scale of truth by which he lives—oh, *he* lives!
All the birds of Chelsea come to him, riotous
　　In his presence, for no milder motives

Could they find on the face of any land
　　Than on his countenance. But something else
Disturbs me, as if an hundred thousand
　　Yeas could be silenced by one Nay that dwells

Hidden in a heart. Does doubt make a monk?
　　Bend nearer, let me whisper my query:
What is this denial that gnaws? Be blunt,
　　Tell me, is all we are mere embroidery

Of the spirit? What moves us in the end?
　　I see a great thirst for perfection,
Supreme ambitiousness, in certain men,
　　As though we could do what cannot be done.

Why is our Thomas so intolerant
　　Of himself? He cannot gain but by grace,
And that is not given for incessant
　　Suffering—it is not ours to purchase.

But why should this pen tremble in my hand?
　　There is an awful silence in my ears—
I flood with apprehension—I stand
　　Before a doubt, which fades and disappears

33

When I draw close. It shifts, I shift. I move,
  And cannot live for very long in one place—
I am not steadfast like More, I disprove
  My own contentions: they are no solace.

I could almost wish now to be convinced,
  Like that silly priest from Louvain, and go
With him, the poor fool, to seek the province
  Of Utopia, that we might echo

There the hollow imitations of Christ,
  And so win them to a most divine life.
But in these moods I sound an atheist.
  Dear Hutten, it's my stomach's invective

Against my culpable neglect of health.
  You are an undeserved friend so to bear
My afflictions with me, and may my death
  Bring us both some peace. It is an affair

Worth consideration, yes? But, enough
  Considering today—my animus
Is well vented. I need only one breath
  More to say, I remain, yours, Erasmus.

AUSTRALIA: FIVE POEMS

SOUTH YARRA

You remember the slant of light, how the morning
sun angles in, dividing the room: this, the joy
of the not yet begun; that, the shadow of the dream.
On the table, the cyclamen luxuriates.

By noon, the blank wall in the study is blinding—
an Aegean intensity looming above the desk—
and the cypress outside casts a net of shadows
on the floor, as doubts catch at your feet.

Later, your book is illumined by the sun—
an understanding you have with the afternoon:
its decline an accommodation, its bar of light
on the page a blessing. You rise with the evening.

PLASTIC EXPLOSIVE IN
TOORAK ROAD

The shop assistant steps up into the window bay
demurely, pauses, and begins to undress
the mannikin. Smiling at her thoughts, self-
conscious in exposure, she notices she
is noticed. The man in the car is also young,
but his smile is forced, his look abstract.
Nakedness is force. She begins dismembering:
first an arm, then another, lies on the ground.
With a tenderness that perplexes her, she holds
a head in her lap. She could almost cry.

PHILLIP ISLAND

This is an alien shore, and that a foreign sea,
   whose deep-green water—nothing like the sky—
folds in upon the strand, with mist on its back, and
   an interstice of foam. Out on the rocks,
offshore, the seals, like wet rocks, wait as
   the grey and wounded clouds drag wings of rain.
We have tasted the wind for hours, smelled its salty
   mixture of sea and land, imagining
late summer islands of remembrance, calling
   to mind nothing but some recreated
flow of created time, days of brave departures.
   And this is not of the moment, having
no use, no immediate connection to life,
   but the sheer chance encounter with something
continuous, distance made more distant by rain
   on the water, whenever the sea storms.
And no misgivings could mar this moment—
   the very waves, beating the shore, withdraw
in foaming undertow and carry with the tide:
   exhausted, redeemed; exhausted, redeemed.
It is the fever of our lives that we
   compel the sudden changes and all the while
ache with an alien solitude, knowing what
   changes us flows from a sea beyond change.

COFFEE CUPS & CHINA TEA

Wider than you can believe, under the long span
of the Pacific Highway Bridge, the Hawkesbury River
        flows through my coffee cup. It is nothing less
than spectacular. I am moved by the grandeur of the
        steep hills, the elaborate brightness of sunlight
on water, the wind given shape by sailboats plunging
        among waves. I look up. My companion has not
noticed. He is drinking green China tea, placid as a
        bowl of white rice. I look down, hoping to prolong
the lull in conversation, thinking he will not notice
        now, without the rich dark stimulus of coffee.
I take a sip, but the wind only blows harder, squalling
        among the boats. There are cries of exhilaration
and fear, of happiness, along the intriguing
        estuary. I look up. My friend has noticed.
He says he prefers green tea, the coffee is so strong here.
        I can see what he means. Visions, he says, are so
common these days in Carlton. Even the Café Paradiso
        moved out. My friend prefers memories—he says
China tea reminds him of Milwaukee in the '60s.
        Still, this cup of coffee is exciting—and would
make a good memory? He says no, the time for memories
        is over, the past has already happened. He shudders
to look at my cup, just as a cloud bank drags shadows
        over Broken Bay and the air turns cool on the water.
I see the boats heading for the shore. It's time to go.
        I drain the cup, tasting a little syrup of sugar
at the bottom. What a bright day outside! And such a wind.

THE BACK BEACH AT BLAIRGOWRIE

Along cliff heights, among tea-trees,
we hurried, as in fear of the wind's
saltations, seeking out the canopies
of rock below, where the shoreline winds.

We came to terms with declivities
of interchange, where land and sea
and air converge, where, leeward, lees
of worried stone were left in fee.

We found shelter on the sand and watched
as the waves stormed across the bar.
Etched, the cliffs stood out on their watch,
and a gull shone fixed as a star.

Freedom, we thought, but the wind blew sand
in our mouths; then beauty was our plea,
but sea-spray, stinging, flew up the strand.
So we turned to hear the song of the sea.

But the sea was urging its endless refrain:
recurrence, recurrence
is all we know of loss and gain—
pull of the undertow, drag of the currents.

No—we returned, and the cliffs re-echoed
the echoing cry, we know
human time: the brief hello, hallowed
good-bye, the finite yes, final no.

But the sea still urged its cold refrain,
as we moved to climb the cliff above,

where fear and the wind were all the strain
and tea-trees innocent of love.

YORK CYCLE: FOUR POEMS

YORK MINSTER

By the city walls the cathedral ministers to pain,
As the Seven Sisters refuse to glow in the dulling light.
Women in scarves, the poor in spirit, hold close
Their collars, clutching at the throat of compassion.

The traffic moves in deliberation and drizzle, as lights
Flicker in second stories, in the unfurnished flats.
Somewhere, equivocally, a cry. Was it joy?
The women catch. Was it loneliness? They look down

The street to where the brass railing gleams
On the Archbishop's stairs; his door a ceremonial red.
The women lower like clouds that cannot lift above
The rooftops; they would give anything to dissipate

In an outpour of tears, but cannot let themselves go
For all the world. In the Minster, they are excavating
The foundations—the geology of their church reveals
A Roman ruin. They have built upon peace, upon a cry

In the wilderness; a monkish pallor of dust envelopes
The tombs. Bells sound in the muffled air, people hurry
Across the street. Vespers. Below, a workman leans
On his shovel, wiping away the sweat of centuries.

MYSTERY PLAYS

Every third year the cycle is played out:
the world is created, condemned and delivered.
Noah drifts ashore, badgered by his wife,
Herod rages and the Innocents are slaughtered.
Less than divine, someone poses as Christ, while
the Last Judgement is passed by the audience.
In the garden, the peacocks are unlovely;
the River Ouse slides by, murky as guilt;
tickets strew the grounds like promises;
the ineffable becomes the insufferable.
Here, mystery plays no role in celebrating
its passing; the city forgets more than it
can recall. When it's over, the stage shell
gapes like a former self, called up by a memory
you cannot place. As the gardens revert
to innocence, to children, the old reclaim
their benches in the unremarkable shade.

ST. PETER'S SCHOOL

The House Master stares out the window
on the balcony: rain. He overhears the mockery
of his cruel, risible boys. He will not marry.
On the floor below, the former Master dozes
in his chair near the fire. He never
married, never outgrew the growing up.
The boys delight in their capacities,
they can cure anyone of compassion.

In the abandonment of night,
asleep in steel beds lined up like barracks,
they dream of crows flapping in black gowns.
In morning chapel the singing is desultory,
as pew by pew their voices falter, as if
word by word they are emptied of song.
The painted boss above the sacristy door
gleams with the crossed keys of St. Peter.

THE CITY WALLS

Along the embankment, below the walls,
bulbs bloom in spring, tidy and on time.
Across the way, a woman's voice calls out,

"This is York. This is York," as the trains all
arrive ahead of schedule. That is York.
Beyond the walls is also York, but the visitor

can't visit the invisible: Rowntree's Chocolate
Factories hide the workers by day, and
city walls obscure their suburbs at night.

People come to walk the walls, but the view
is always inward: there the River Ouse, there
the Guildhall, Minster, Lord Mayor's mansion.

They climb the battlements of Bootham Bar,
admire quaint Walmgate Bar; delight
in the names Fishergate, Micklegate, Gillygate.

The Shambles is always popular in spring,
a wayward street celebrating conformity.
But the city walls are what people remember,

built on a human scale, though no human can
scale them. Braced against the past, as if
protecting the springtime of the city,

they crenelate York's empirical sky.

POSTCARDS

CITIES

Everywhere a river and a bridge, a coastline,
some clear waterway blue with the sky
to lead us through the picture
of where you are—or have been, for how
will we ever catch up, having been left behind?
We hardly glance at these snapshots of absence—
impatient, we read what seems to picture you best:
out of all the cities of words, you pass on
what you have taken in, and little boulevards
of phrases become the avenues of approach.
We search the sound of what you say,
we wish to come close to what you see, and perhaps
then, it is the picture after all that says the most:
always present in its momentary world, as
the arrested water forever flows, and in
receiving it, though dated and cancelled as foreign,
it is like some bridge we have built over all
distances, or like the blue river itself, or
the remarkable sea that took you away,
connects you to our shore, and keeps you away.

ICONS

Stone, wood, paint and plaster—there is no
medium these cards cannot reduce to say
what all along they were meant to mean:
We are here, and you are with us.
But now I take them all for dreams,
the shining statue, the bleeding crucifix—
what they mean is what they do not say:
the raised palms and bowed head, the peasant
kneeling at the portal, the stone figure firm
upon its post, each in its way a posture taken
for the life given, the life returned.
And among these cards and icons of the world,
I think mostly now of the long return.

EPILOGUE

And as he walked then in a city of many people—
the intermittent rain insisting upon its presence now
as sheer downpour—he knew there would always be
that day when the light with the coloration of distance
brought everything nearer, made it all seem possible,
even necessary: a pouring of himself out of himself.

III

AUBADE

I, friend to the morning, wake
as she wakes, discreet in the light that comes
before the light of the sun—
dawn, dew, steam rising at the touch,
over fields, on roofs, my breathing
the mirror of the morning, ache of day.
Sweet morning: unremembered, unleavened,
green in the pale light, shining brook in
the mountain of years, white water washing
the old night, the dark panes glowing.
Doors to the day open in light:
my room, the messenger of dreams, arbiter
of sorrow, friend to the morning. Praise
the matin laudings, praise to my friends—
come, friend of the morning, wake
as she wakes, sing her song of rising.

COMMUTE

Always in those trips by car
there was a sense of wishing for what
was not yet: morning's appointments,
a quick lunch, conversations
in the afternoon, the ride back.
And when the sun rose and the speeding air
glittered, the talk again turned
to older travels, other travails.
And always it seemed we had passed that point
before, and the landscapes converged
to a simple prospect, a single wish:
that everything recurring for us might end,
the coming and going over the same ground,
that we might split the cost of turning
forward to begin again—payment
in exchange for all we may have changed.

ROOMS

i

I am standing holding a letter I
do not understand: it is from home and
has been forwarded to this inn, to this room.
The room moves, the curtains sway, I sit down.
Outside the birds make sounds I recognize,
evening songs, grace notes near the cathedral wall.
It is summer here. Someone is looking for me.

ii

This is my study, on the balcony:
below is where we sit, above my wife
weaves and reweaves. Sometimes I lie on the floor
and watch the sky meet the hill in back and
send down the little stream white in winter.
Once I thought it was time's emblem, but now
it flows into my sight and washes my eyes.

iii

Somebody lives here, in bed, and will die too late.
I amuse her and try to be brave, trying
to be. The drapes are closed against the light,
but the sun suffuses the room and glows in the
corner, quiet as the hushed rustle of bedclothes.
I think that I too should lie here and give
up the weight of my bones to the substance of air.

iv

This is a foreign room, in Florence, over
a busy street. The cries below seem close.
I am not alone, but lie on the bed face down,

suffering the truth that I do not love
this girl bound to me through my own self-love.
The ceiling is the floor, and the walls exchange
through the emptiness of a callow heart.

v

Our first house, here, called Amity Road, seems
blessed in spontaneity, for joys come
faster and live like green ferns on air, sustained
by the happy chance of happiness, before
the dull average of days yellows the walls.
This is the living room we recreate,
the space we make for each other, each time.

vi

I have woken early, startled by the
dislocation of my memory, and
remember suddenly I am back in my
childhood's house, where the smells and noises stay
forever: the birthplace of all my dreams, where all
my failings found a home. How the doorknob
turns, the light switch clicks, has determined me.

vii

This room is empty, shadeless, bright and cold,
vacant as the eye that stares in the mirror:
a room I have come to recognize each time.
I cannot fill it, I seal it against the wind.
Yet there are days I seek it out, to ask
of it my future, to tell it about my past.
It is the first room of the house I build.

RAIN

It has rained all day, and the daylilies,
exhausted, hang in an orange profusion of repose,
while the rain comes down all day.
Is it summer? You would not know
for all the rain: it could be any season,
any corner of time, where the long day leans
to an even longer evening. How the afternoon
lingers in rain—or is it summer standing still
that lets the sky release its voice
in a breathless downpour of wellaway words?
Midsummer: there is no turning back,
only over and over: the days, the weather,
ourselves in the night, restless in the heat,
turning over again the earliest memories of days.
Steadily the rain comes, with wind, then goes,
while the storm stays. And still we sit here listening
by the glass doors, as if waiting with the world
for some ancient ceaseless christening.

THE WAY

There was much that was obvious to him
in what came together, how the obverse
of joy—that sad empty echo—fulfilled
the premonitions of completeness, each
day bringing what the last left behind:
the other view, the possibility shunned,
the weather changing out of complacency.
Hear the geese out in the back at night,
their stark music a measure of coldness
descending; listen to the dry leaves
blown in the noon sun, a welcomed
warmth, an utterance wishing to obviate
the deepening frost, the pre-dawn cold—
it goes in that way, something gained
at whatever price its dearness demands.
But the coming together, moving like geese
in formation falling, winding up and on,
it's so certain, so much a matter of
necessity, that you hardly ask why
the leaves fall, or the birds depart, or
why these glorious days filled with fire
burn in the joyful heart, the house of pain.

UNANSWERED QUESTIONS

Even her yes was a way of saying no,
as if nothing could be more agreeable
than the denial of everything. And did it not
affirm, all the same, her willingness
to be exactly who she was? Contrariety
herself. And yet she was not disagreeable—
no, even the waving of the wind through
her black hair seemed the answering
caress of amiable thoughts.

                        Still, there was
nothing to ask for: we knew our minds,
and had the conscience of what each other
knew, or might have forgot, or would
recover in the reflection of themselves
shining through the irrevocable past.

She could not be held answerable
for the doubts that played across
her face—like shadows that move about
when the silence of the trees declines
into dappled shade at your feet.
The sunlight was passed over.

                            But when she
bent over to play then with the cat,
she was a question suddenly—the shape
of indecision that throws you back
upon yourself—for she was something sought,
something unrevealed. And I waited
out the hiatus of those years
to know—how to know?—the final reply.

A HOUSE IN VERMONT

It was a path that many years before had led
to a place that once had been nothing,
was now almost nothing, but a place
in time where once a life was lived.
It was a house then, or was it a village?
I see it from a distance, through the uncertain
light of the forest: though no one lives there
now, to descend the hill and cross the stream,
to enter, would be premature. It is a question
of timing—so often a matter of moments—
as when we make space out of time and
inhabit a sense of life lived. Closer,
look, the leaves around it dance on the trees,
the wind is happy through the overgrown garden.
Nothing wild there, but our bewilderment
makes it so. There is more to see,
there is ever more to see: this house is a village,
long and large, it wanders along the hillside,
every addition is a house itself, and the impulse
to build, to make more than is natural, more
than any man could die to, seems to find voice
in the uppermost rafters. It is the wind again,
and all the flowers are perennial in their approval.
Go back. The path leads up and winds down to
another kind of village, where disconnected
dwellings stand and shape their common ground:
the green square that defines their world of
separate lives lived together, where all
the people know one another, and even at times
consider as they walk the green paths how
the lives of people are of the very same life,
how it comes and goes and seems like change.
And if, by chance, one were to come upon

this path, with branches in his face
and roots and vines about his feet, if,
let's say, that person was you, and your day
had been like most others: you are tired, you
are depended upon for many things, but here
you find how the green forest refreshes, that
you are content to walk slowly, to take it
all in—will you too come to the abandoned house
and see it as the ruin of a promise, or
as something fulfilled and given back, piece
by piece, to the source of growth, which is decay,
which is, in the end, nothing but life lived?
Even so, you would not stay: a pastoral world is
forever past, and the future brings back the present
again for us to face and know it as ours—
it is the one path we walk to the end.

SNOW FIELDS

In the back lot, above where the stream
fans out, searching for its lost embankment,
someone tried growing spruce trees one year
for Christmas. The field would have nothing
of it and stunted them, excepting a few
that found dry pockets in the deep black-dirt.
It was all swamp once, drained by Poles and
Germans, who knew bottomland, and how
to value the worthless, the disdained.

Now frozen, it's easy to walk on the low
fields, and in the marsh, where cattails
had waved in defiance. In the afternoon,
the old man from across the way comes down
through the woods and on to our land.
He is hunting rabbits. He is deaf, almost.
His beagle hound wails on the scent,
and he follows by sight: shoots at
a flushed bird. His aim is of no purport.

The old man has always done this, since
anyone can remember—it is who he is:
he makes a claim upon our property
and our neighbor's, moving beyond
respect for boundaries and fences,
looking for openings, clearings—
finding the frozen stream that
finally releases him into the
freedom of the snow fields.

PREPARING FOR THE PAST

Walking on the beach—we have done this
before—we are preparing for the past.
It is here already: the sky is enormous
in our memory, the ocean swirls in our palms.

Dreaming of a future passing before us:
we take photographs that fade, exposed.
We are patient with the wind as it blows
in our faces—its naiveté is touching:

it plays like time's child with the loosening
sand. We are not fooled by the tree limbs
blown ashore: there is nothing emblematic about
storm debris: the past has yet to happen—

these are figments of presence. We are not
startled by reversals: we know the arbitrary
leaps of time—how, like the wind, it runs
this way and that—how it laughs, like a child,

to whirl on one spot. Closer than before,
before there was before, it begins much later,
when we turn and say: "We were the waves, green
and white, the sand, pale yellow—the horizon

held us while the wind rejoiced—we were
the blue of sky, the red sandstone of cliffs,
we sang of desire, we remember it now."
This is now. It is gone. We prepare for the past.

FIRE ON THE MOUNTAIN

So close in the woods, so early in the day,
though the rain has left, it stays:
the ground gives way, the mists drift.

On the runnelling road, you listen:
that noise in the forest, like a fire
in the fireplace. It is not fire,

it is the wake of the rain dying out:
the high branches and attendant leaves
shed the running water from green tiers

down to greener tiers, to the ground.
Drips crackle in the stillness—a sound heard
as from a distance. Distance: a moment's

motif—for there is no distance between us:
I speak to you here as to myself, and what
could be further from the truth than

distance from you? Yet you are not here,
you are not here. No rain, no fire—
not presences. Mists burn off, leaf-light

dazzles the clearing. *Fire on the mountain*—
what evasion, distrust, absorption and pride
always turn aside: the speech of self;

the final fire I give you.

A MOMENT'S NOTICE

The blue edge of a cloud declines into gray,
day fades from the winter's window, silhouettes
vie with the shadows reflected from within,
as inside is outside, an illusory world: time
to draw the curtain, turn on the lamps.

It is early afternoon, on the third day of the story,
in the painting above my desk. The summer light
trapped in the oils, plays on the surface of the stream.
On the other side of the field, beyond the willow, he
has just entered the gray house with the green roof.

The procedures of evening are the repetitions of day:
we live in the mirror world of our waking, the crystal
refractions, the prison of our prism. From down the road,
the house lit up is one more ship on a calm night.
Below, the boiler kicks on, moving us towards our destination.

It is only half-painted, the story unfinished, quite
abandoned really: the splotch of white and green foregrounds
the illusion, hinting at the anti-climax to come.
We can only imagine how the ending will go, and hope that
the hero, when the moment comes, will be equal to himself.

It has just happened. You noticed, of course. It's odd,
how few times in the long day we are available. The phone
rings, we're not there, just a voice in a machine, recording
messages. Someone stops by, hello, good-bye, we turn
around and there we are: the other story, the other day.

In the lower right, spreading out into the center,
the shadow deepens and threatens to envelop all
but the frame. His story cannot possibly be

over: the subtle highlights of red, the green
luminosity, admit of no deferral, no completion.

It takes but a moment's notice, and we are ready.
Our bags, for a long time now, have been packed,
the passport in the drawer up to date. What remains
to take leave, is to find a reason for leaving,
to make up some plausible story of our need.

On the fourth day, he was seen departing the house—
the road, only a streak of a suggestion, leading
over what might be called a bridge. The field in light,
beyond the central hill, can be taken for a sign
of the joy he must have felt opening before him.

STELLAR JUNK

The first to return were the satellites,
like so many shooting stars in the fall air;
later, fragments of a space station, detritus
from failures we had ignored or forgotten.
And it dawned on us that a world-wide
depression had settled over the young.
Scientists were puzzled, people were afraid.
    O Lord, they said, give us another vision.

Soon everything slowed down. New Yorkers
shuffled in the street, cars stalled out on hills.
And then one day, a violin floated down
like a balloon, then someone's lost keys, then
single pairs of socks, earrings, gloves, engagement rings.
And everything of value we thought we had lost
rained upon us, made us feel whole again,
and we cried for the joy of it, and we laughed
for the simple terror of not knowing why.
    O Lord, we shouted, give us another vision.

But the world was cluttered with memory,
people walked about as if stunned in a weather
of weariness, their eyelids weighed down.
And so it came to pass: in daylight, one by one,
like planes landing at LaGuardia, they returned.
We thought they were angels, transfigurations
in robes—but saints, martyrs came, shrouded,
Lazarus and the prophets, mystics, Church fathers.
They crumpled into the dust at our feet.
Some wore smiles, others the grimace of death-masks.
We could not bear to lift them, their prophecy fulfilled.
    O Lord, we cried, give us another vision.

By then we had fallen to our knees,
our lips mumbling involuntary prayers;
we watched the skies, knowing what would come.
The heaviness in our hearts drew him down.
In a glory, a halo, he took days to arrive—
we grew accustomed to his atomic light.
He was falling so slowly, head over barefoot heels,
his garments flapping in the celestial air.
He landed face down, legs broken.
No one approached, until the children came
and gathered him; then we carried the body
to a cross we had prepared on a hill.
The wounds had never healed—that job was easy—
though many turned away for the nailing.
No one cast lots, no pieces of silver could suffice.
After three days we took him down—
he had the weight of our own encumbrance.
    O Lord, we prayed, give us another vision.

The tides are running higher, sea birds inhabit
the forest. We are leaden with acceptance.
For a long time we didn't notice, but now,
more huge than the sun in the sky, visible
all day, we see the moon coming down,
and all the seas are rising to meet it.
We hope it will end there. We are looking
forward to uncreation, to beyond our own time.
    O Lord, Lord, we give you our vision.

BIOGRAPHICAL NOTE

PAUL KANE was born in the village of Cobleskill, in upstate New York, in 1950. Educated at Yale College, he has also received graduate degrees from Yale University and from the University of Melbourne, Australia, where he was a Fulbright scholar in 1984. He has worked in a variety of occupations, including teaching and administration, bookselling, carpentry, landscaping, and textile restoration. Kane is poetry editor for *Antipodes* (a North American journal of Australian literature), and is currently engaged in teaching and research at Yale. He lives with his wife, Tina, in Warwick, New York.

THE BRAZILLER SERIES OF POETRY
Richard Howard, General Editor